The Missing Amulet

Jane Langford
Illustrated by Jenny Gregory

Rigby

Keno put his fishing pole into the water again. He loved fishing, and he and his friend Kim often spent their Saturdays trying to catch fish through a hole in the ice.

Keno sat and fiddled with the amulet around his neck as he waited for the fish to bite.

Suddenly, Keno gasped in horror. The string broke, and his precious amulet slid into the icy water. "Oh no!" he cried. He plunged his arm into the water and grasped at the sinking amulet, but it was no good. The little stone seal that his father had so lovingly carved was gone.

"What's wrong?" called Kim. He dropped his pole and came running over the ice toward Keno.

"It's my amulet," said Keno. "I dropped it into the water."

Kim edged carefully toward the hole. He peered into the dark, murky depths.

"Was it important?" Kim asked.

"Yes!" said Keno. "My father carved it. He said that the Inuit people have always worn amulets. They bring good luck."

Kim nodded. "I know," he said, "but it's only a piece of stone. Come away from the edge of the hole. The ice might break."

"No, it won't," said Keno. "I've got to find my amulet."

Keno bent over the hole and peered in.
At first he could see nothing, but then he gasped
in amazement. A seal was swimming just below
the surface, and the amulet was caught around
its nose.

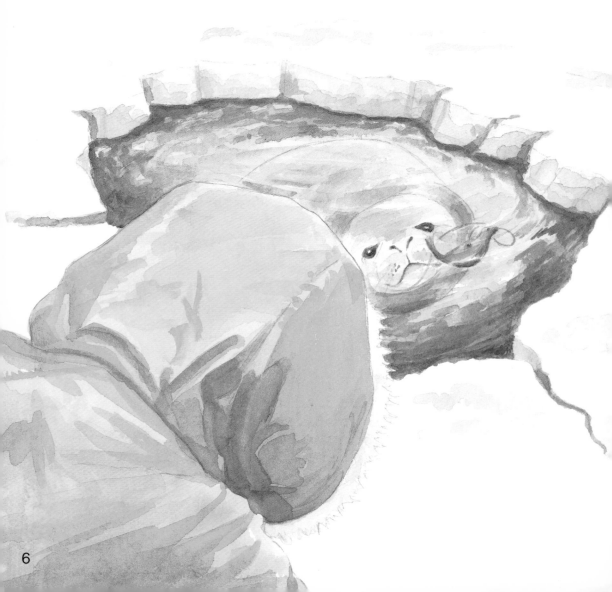

"I can see the amulet!" yelled Keno.

Keno leaned further and further over the hole.

Suddenly, Kim heard the ice crack. "Watch out!" he yelled. "The ice is cracking!"

Keno stood up and took a step back from the hole, but it was too late. The ice broke.

SPLASH! Keno fell into the freezing water. The cold hit him like a sledgehammer.

Kim gasped with horror. "I've got to get him out of there or he'll die!" Kim lay flat on the ice. He caught hold of Keno's fishing pole and plunged it into the water. "Grab hold of that!" he yelled.

Keno grabbed at the pole but he missed. Kim tried again. It was no good. Keno was having trouble keeping his head above the water.

Kim stood up and waved his arms at the distant group of houses.

"Help!" he cried. "Help!"

In the distance, Keno's father saw Kim. He realized something was wrong and jumped onto his snowmobile.

Kim cried with relief as he heard the distant hum of the snowmobile's engine. But when he looked down again, Keno had disappeared.

"No!" shouted Kim.

He edged toward the hole and peered into the water. Tears filled his eyes as he realized that Keno was gone.

"Keno!" he shouted. "Keno!" Kim waved his arms at Keno's father in despair, but he was still a long way off.

Suddenly, Kim heard a furious snort. It was
the seal! It poked its head out of the water.
Kim brushed aside his tears and reached for
the amulet that was still caught on the seal's nose.

Then Kim saw something else in the water. He reached down again and touched something cold and icy. It was Keno's fingers! Kim grabbed hold of Keno and held on tight.

The snowmobile was very close now. Keno's father stopped the engine and raced over toward Kim. He caught hold of Keno, and they pulled him onto the ice.

Keno coughed and sputtered. He lay on the ice and slowly opened his eyes. He saw his father.

"I've lost the amulet," he said. "It was supposed to bring me luck."

"It did!" said Kim, pressing the amulet into Keno's hand. "You're alive!"